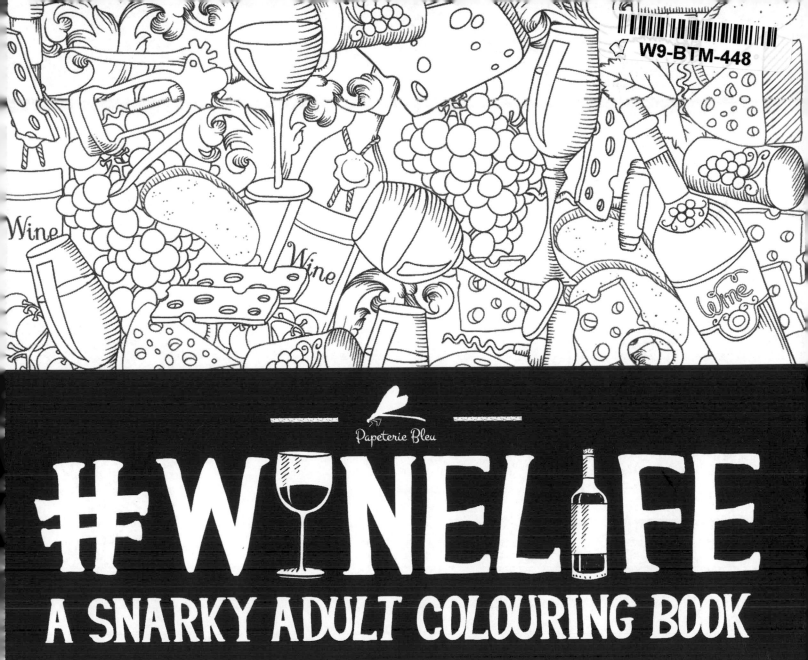

Papeterie Bleu

#WINELIFE

A SNARKY ADULT COLOURING BOOK

Illustrated by Micaela

ISBN-13: 978-1-64001-019-2
ISBN-10: 1-64001-019-X

FREE DOWNLOAD

www.papeteriebleu.com/winelifeEN

YOUR DOWNLOAD CODE: WINE6765

 @papeteriebleu

 Papeterie Bleu

MY BLOOD TYPE IS MERLOT BUT I'M A UNIVERSAL RECIPIENT

paste LABEL here

paste LABEL here

paste LABEL here

paste LABEL here

paste LABEL here

paste LABEL here

I'm a wine ENTHUSIAST. The more WINE I DRINK the more ENTHUSIASTIC I become

paste
LABEL
here

Keep your Friends CLOSE
Keep your Vino CLOSER

paste LABEL here

paste LABEL here

paste
LABEL
here

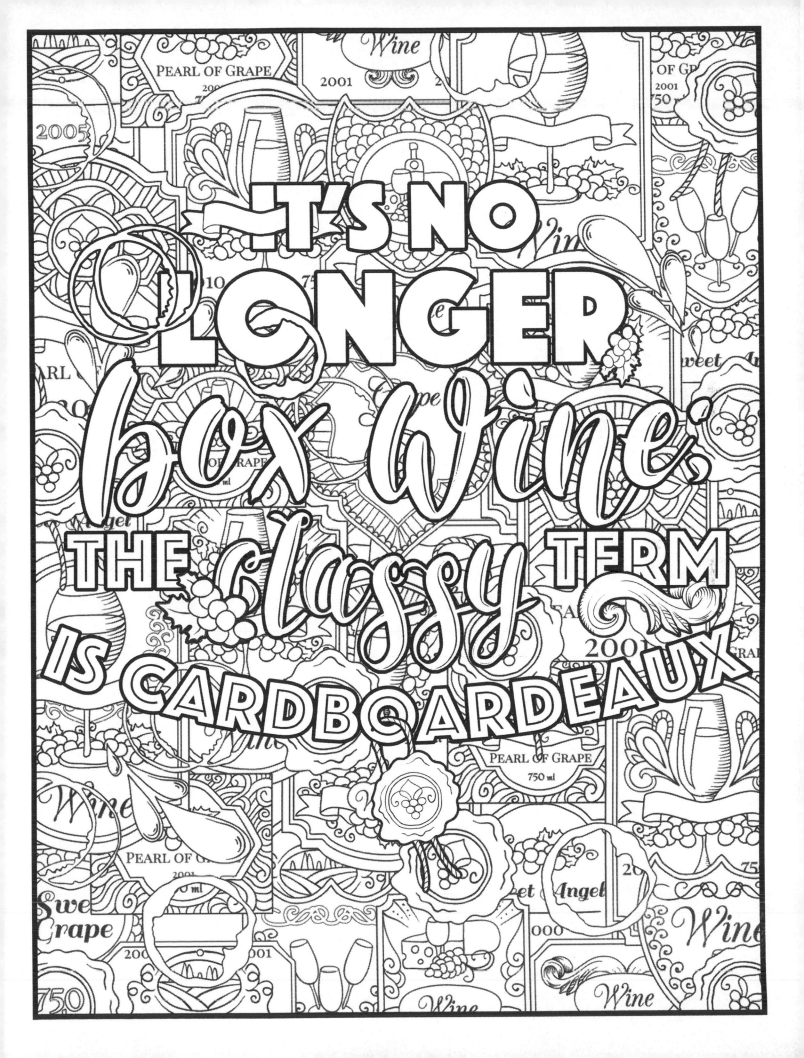

paste LABEL here

I LIKE TO Cook WITH WINE Sometimes I EVEN ADD it to the FOOD

paste LABEL here

paste
LABEL
here

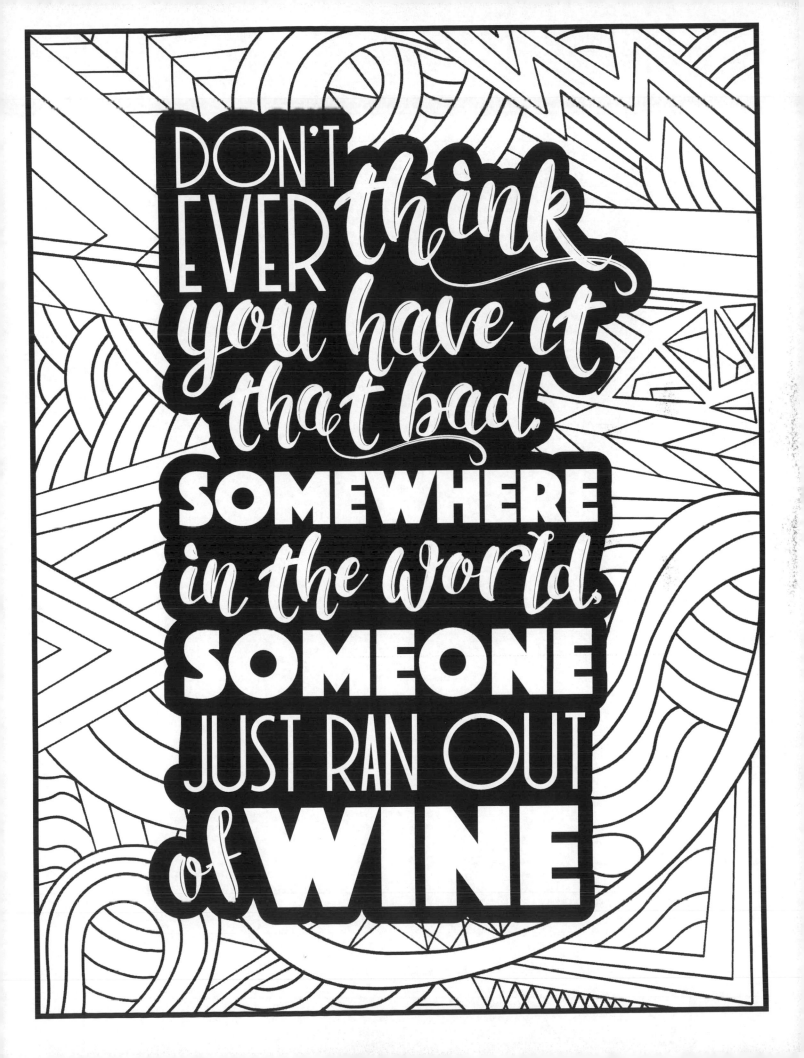

paste LABEL here

paste LABEL here

paste LABEL here

People who WONDER whether the GLASS IS HALF EMPLY OR HALF FULL are missing the point. The glass is REFILLABLE

paste LABEL here

paste LABEL here

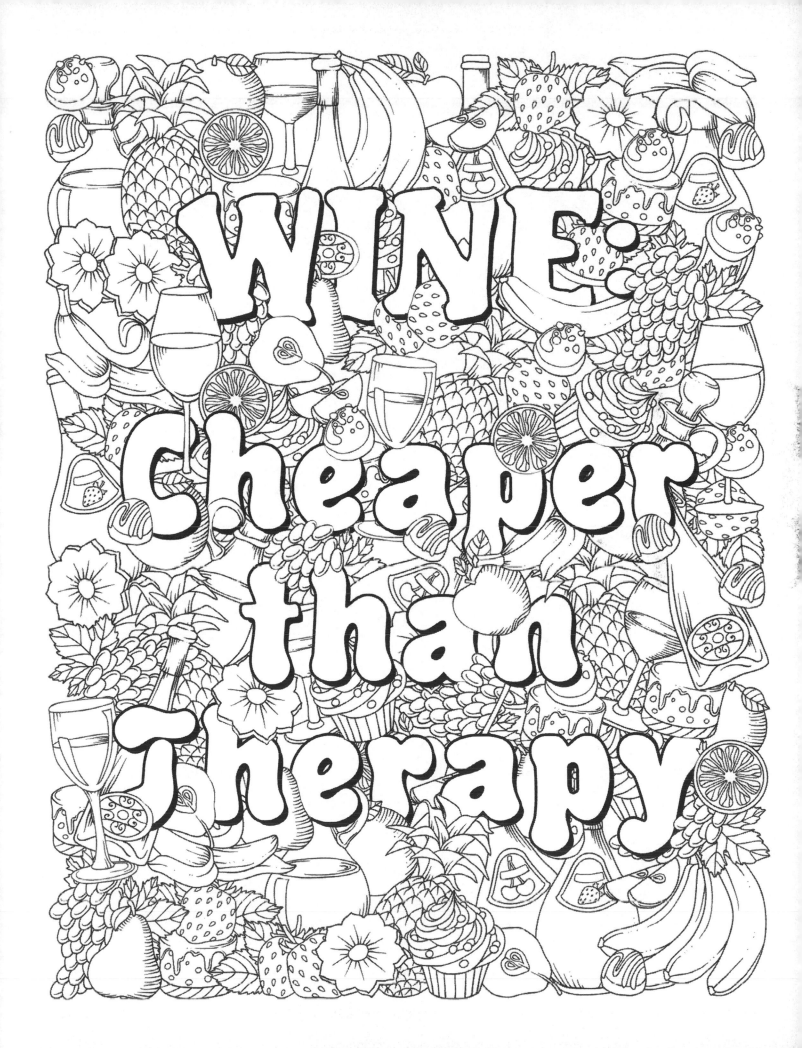

paste LABEL here

paste LABEL here

TECHNICALLY YOU'RE not DRINKING alone

if YOUR DOG is at home

paste LABEL here

paste
LABEL
here

paste LABEL here

I ENJOY THE 1 other GLASS OF WINE each night FOR THE HEALTH BENEFITS. & GLASSES ARE FOR WITTY comebacks & flawless DANCE MOVES!

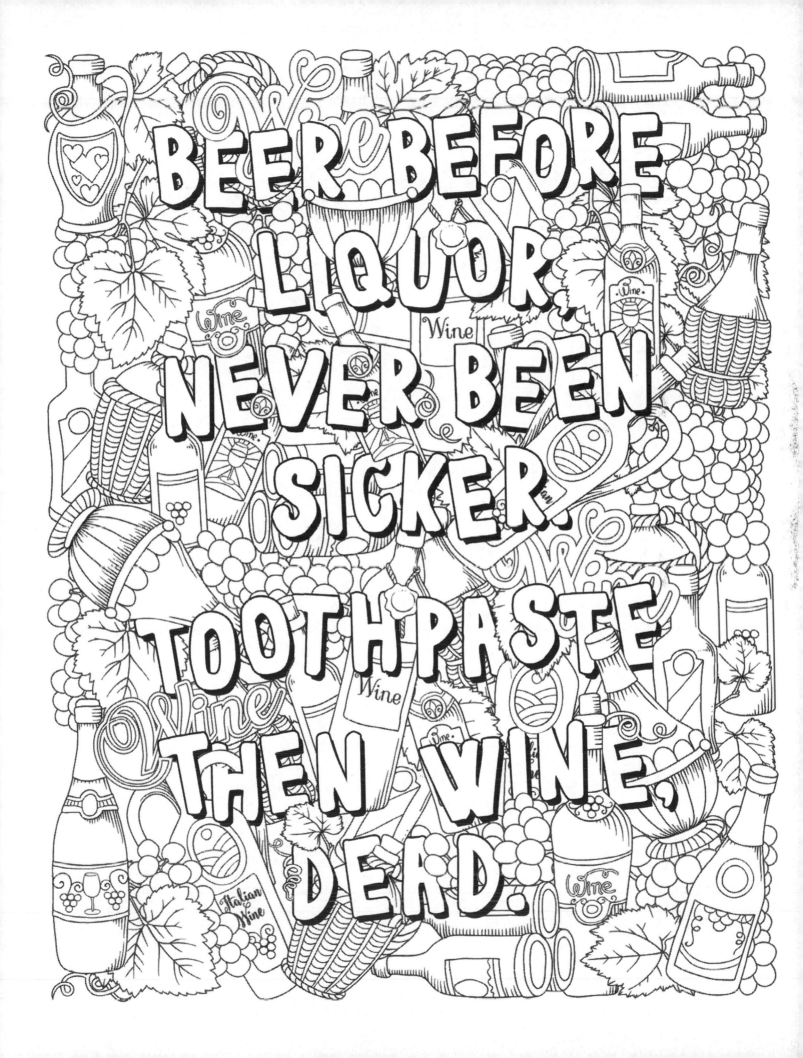

paste LABEL here

paste
LABEL
here

paste
LABEL
here

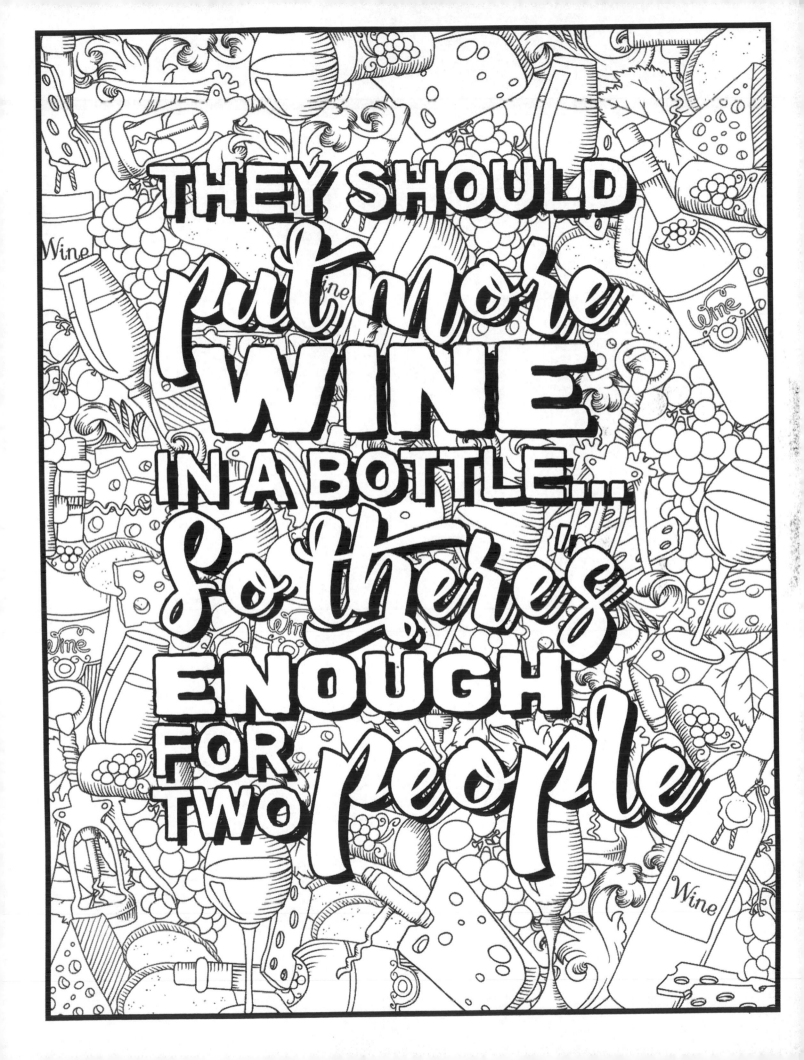

paste
LABEL here

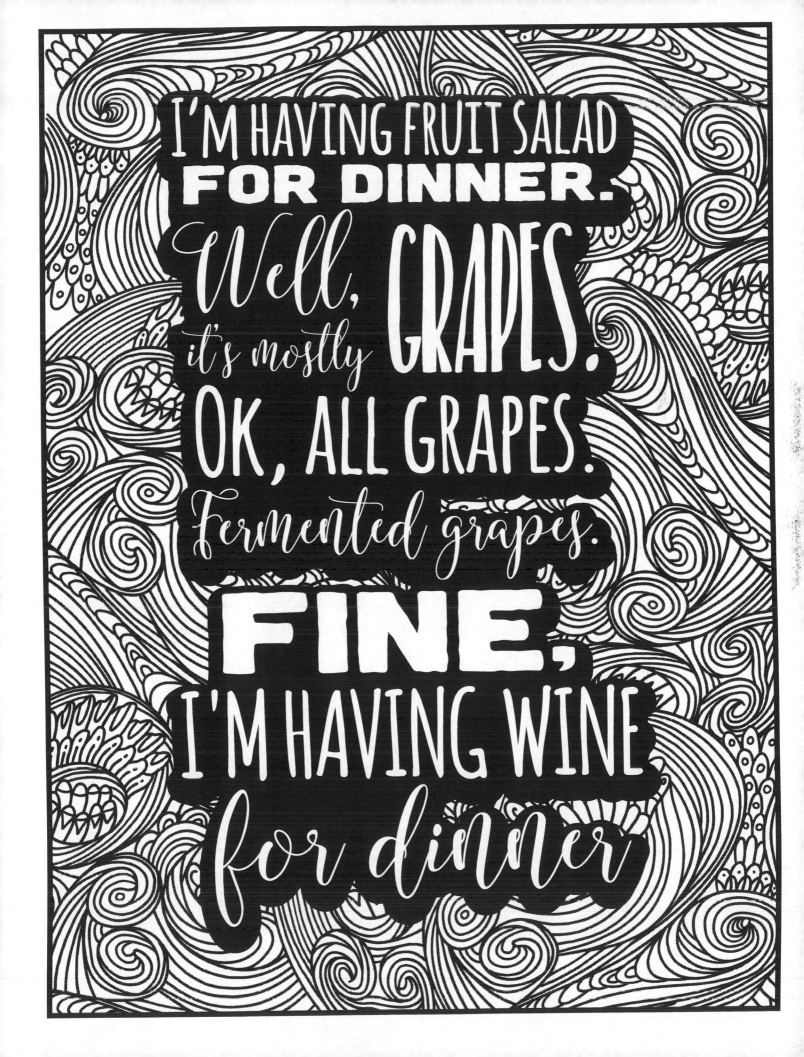

paste LABEL here

BE SURE TO FOLLOW US ON SOCIAL MEDIA FOR THE LATEST NEWS, SNEAK PEEKS, & GIVEAWAYS

@PapeterieBleu

Papeterie Bleu

@PapeterieBleu

ADD YOURSELF TO OUR MONTHLY NEWSLETTER FOR FREE DIGITAL DOWNLOADS AND DISCOUNT CODES

www.papeteriebleu.com/newsletter

CHECK OUT OUR OTHER BOOKS!

www.papeteriebleu.com

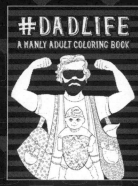

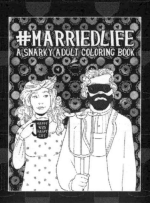

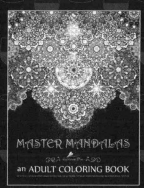

CHECK OUT OUR OTHER BOOKS!

www.papeteriebleu.com

    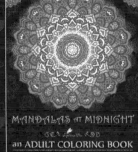

    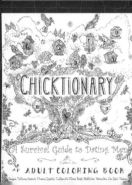

CHECK OUT OUR OTHER BOOKS!

www.papeteriebleu.com

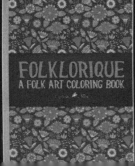 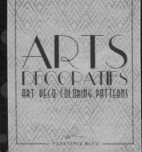 

Made in the USA
Middletown, DE
08 August 2017